T0132421

CARELESS

RAMBLES

CARELESS RAMBLES

by John Clare

A SELECTION OF HIS POEMS

CHOSEN AND ILLUSTRATED

by Tom Pohrt

WITH A FOREWORD

by Robert Hass

COUNTERPOINT

BERKELEY

ISBN: 978-1-61902-315-4

Cover and interior design by David Bullen

Printed in the United States of America

COUNTERPOINT
2560 Ninth Street, Suite 318
Berkeley, CA 94710
www.counterpointpress.com

for Isabel and Carmen

TABLE OF CONTENTS

PREFACE

I stumbled on the name John Clare a few years ago in a book review. It was in the opening pages of Christopher Hitchins book *God Is Not Great*: "If you read John Clare's imperishable rural poems you will catch the music of what I mean to convey." Imperishable rural poems. Reading this I felt an immediate and overwhelming impulse to follow the name John Clare. I had heard of this poet. His name was imbedded in my subconscious, but it was not until later that I recalled the sing-song poem Little Trotty Wagtail.

Coming across the Hitchens review and reading that particular sentence was like catching a side-long peripheral glance of a bird in flight, that just as easily could have been missed. I took to my computer to research what I could find of Clare. Before the night was out I felt I knew the direction I was headed in for the next year or so.

> *The path's even covered with insects—each sort*
> *Flock by, crowds in the smiles of the morning to sport:*
> *There's the cricket in brown and his cousin in green,*
> *The grasshopper dancing, and o'er them is seen*
> *The ladybird dressed like a hunter in red,*
> *Creeping out from the blossom with whom she went bed.*
> *So good little girls, now disturb not their play*
> *And you, Freddy, stop till they hop far away,*
> *For to kill them in sport, as many folks will,*
> *And call it a pastime 'tis cruel and ill,*
> *As their lives are as sweet of enjoyment as ours*
> *And they dote like yourselves upon sunshine and flowers.*

Like a Jain monk gently sweeping the floor for insects, so as not to accidently step on them, Clare penned these lines with a deep compassion to identify with the natural world. This empathy with insects, plants and animals is one of the things endearing to Clare's poetry. (In our own household my young daughter and I bottle the stray ant, spider and bee, to remove outdoors.)

The above poem, *The Holiday Walk*, begins;

> *Come, Eliza and Anna, lay by top and ball*
> *And, friendly boy, throw away cart and toys all,*
> *Look about for your hats and dispense with your play,*
> *We'll seek for the fields and be happy today.*

Here, Clare is taking his own children (Eliza, Anna & Freddy) out on a nature walk, but he also taking us along on the ramble, a walk as well perhaps into his own childhood past. His description of the landscape reads as if before the Enclosure Acts, when there were still plenty of open fields and common land around Helpston and the surrounding parishes. From vast sky-scape description of "hawks sailing proud as the clouds" to the flea-glass/microscope intimacy of ants "nimbling about in the grass", we tag along on this happy sojourn.

At heart the poems of John Clare also take me back to when I was much younger, to hot summer days spent wandering fields, inland lakes and woods of my northern Michigan, "Nick Adams" country. Our family spent many summers vacationing in this northern landscape. My parents owned property in an old Anishinabe Indian community situated along a bluff overlooking Lake Michigan. The local farmers were a mix of Irish, English, German, and later Polish. By the early 20th century the logging industry that long defined the economy here had mostly disappeared. Few descendants of the original inhabitants remain. But not long ago an older generation would often leave a wood chair propped against their front door when away from the house. You would see this from a distance and save yourself the walk. A lost civilized touch.

Red and Jack pine, birch, box elder, poplar, maples, Doug

fir, the long lived white cedar, various oaks, beech, and elm along with an abundance of nut bearing trees make up the surrounding forest. The majestic northern white pine (Weymouth pine in Britain) is also found in these woods. I had my favorite climbing trees, a number of old oaks, and an ancient pine that still stands. There were a pair of magnificent elms that grew together in the middle of a field between the bluff and lake. Raspberry bushes surrounded these huge trees. They appeared untouched by Dutch-elm disease, that was responsible for the loss of the big elms that lined the street I grew up on in the city of Flint. These healthy trees were later cut down, for reasons I still can not fathom.

My father was keen on birds and delighted in identifying their calls. This interest extended to his knowledge in identifying trees and the grain in their wood. We had our secret spot for finding elderberries, snapping off bunches to take home, washing and stripping berries from the branches, leaving finger tips stained purple, for pies. We often collected black walnuts, a time-intensive passion with a meager return when we counted the number of eatable nuts retrieved.

I picked mushrooms from deep in the woods and we all hunted for raspberries and blueberries. We kept an open-eye when fresh bear scat was found in the low growing bush. I spent many long hours in solitary observation of nature, for pure enjoyment.

The idea of an illustrated collection of Clare simply came about as I was reading his poems. The superb *John Clare: A Biography* by Jonathan Bate was also an inspiration. A handful of my pen/ink sketches appeared in The John Clare Society Journal in 2009.

There is a wanderlust and a rambling sense of discovery in Clare's poetry, that I wanted to convey with this collection. Clare was such a prolific poet it could not be helped that a number of excellent poems would have to be left out. I picked the poems I liked. This selection is my own.

Tom Pohrt   20th October, 2011

Cambridge is about fifty miles north of London—forty-five minutes now by train. It is another thirty miles north and west—and a world away—to Helpston, the rural village on the edge of the flat fen country of Northamptonshire where John Clare was born in 1793. His mother, a village girl, was illiterate, his father a scarcely literate laborer. The children of itinerant farm workers in that time and place were even less likely to become poets than the children of migrant laborers are in the United States today. John Clare was from birth a "clown," the local dialect word for "peasant," and he grew up to write poems of a freshness and sweetness unlike anything else in English poetry.

His subject was mostly the natural world as he experienced it in the early decades of the nineteenth century. He wrote many poems about walking, about going out and coming back. Snugness was another of his themes, under which there is a subliminal sense of the peril and terror of living. But the surfaces of many of his poems have to do with the happy, endlessly interesting look of things. He knew more about the patterns of rural life than any other English poet, and he was much the best field naturalist among them. His admirers and advocates since his death in 1864 have included Arthur Symons, Edward Thomas, Seamus Heaney, and John Ashbery. And I think he is hardly known to American readers.

There are reasons for this, of course. They have much to do with his origins and the shape of his life. John Clare's mother, whose name was Anne Stimson, was a shepherd's daughter. His father, according to the village story, was the illegitimate son of an itinerant Scots fiddler who had wooed the village clerk's pretty daughter. When the daughter, Alice Clare, John's grandmother, discovered she was pregnant, the fiddler decamped, and when her son was born, Alice gave the boy, Parker, her surname.

Parker Clare became a farm laborer in the village where he was born and in the neighboring villages when he could get work there. He was also a fiddler, and, though not a reader, liked to boast in the public house that he could sing or recite more than a hundred ballads. Parker married Anne Stimson, and so John Clare came into the world.

John Clare's formal education was over by the time he was eleven. At thirteen he had discovered poetry and begun to write it while he worked in the fields and at whatever other forms of day labor came his way, lime-burning, driving cattle, digging and setting hedges. When he was twenty-five, he met a bookseller in the market town of Stamford and through him arranged to have a book of poems published—in London, by the publisher of the young Cockney poet, John Keats. The book, *Poems, Descriptive of Rural Life and Scenery*, was printed in 1820, when Clare was twenty-six years old. It created a small sensation—here was a peasant poet with a thorough knowledge of the rural landscape, a rich sense of local dialect, and an ear trained by reading Spenser and the eighteenth century nature poets, especially Thomson and Cowper. He read the poets of his own time, when he could get his hands on the books: Byron, whom he adored, and Wordsworth and Coleridge, and another rural poet, Robert Bloomfield.

Clare became, briefly, famous. His publisher invited him to London where he met Samuel Coleridge and Charles Lamb and a number of painters and other writers, and then he returned to his own life in Helpston. He married, had seven children, lived in a small cottage with that brood and with his elderly and ailing parents, and continued, intermittently, to find day work as a laborer. His fame helped him for a time in the form of stipends and favors from the local aristocracy, who wanted to see this curiosity that was John Clare, the poet. His entry to their world—through the servant's entrance—gave him friendships with the upper servants and gamekeepers of a couple of the great local families. These new friends shared his passion for ornithology and botany. The relationship with his benefactors was probably more complicated. "I must confess," a Lord Radstock wrote, "that I discover in his character a want of gratitude and proper feeling toward the opulent higher orders which has lower'd him not a little in my opinion."

During those years, roughly 1820 to 1835, poetry poured out of Clare. Three more books of poetry followed the first one, but the world had largely lost interest. The vogue for poetry that Byron and Sir Walter Scott had created was waning and, one imagines, the idea of the peasant poet quickly lost its novelty. His publishers hurried out a second book, *The Village Minstrel, and Other Poems*, a year after the first one. By the time they printed his third book, *The Shepherd's Calendar with Village Stories*, six years later, they were themselves struggling to stay afloat. The fourth and final book, *The Rural Muse*, appeared a decade later, in 1835, after a number of frustrating delays.

Clare also worked, in the midst of his growing family, on various prose projects, natural history mostly, as he tried to find a way to earn a living as a writer. He made several more trips to London—by coach in those days—and was feted by some of the admirers of his poems. He had his portrait painted by a well known painter—a picture of a handsome, blondish young man with delicate features and hazel eyes. He met Hazlitt and de Quincy and Wordsworth. He looked at paintings and went to prizefights. It was an age when boxing—"the fancy," as it was called—was wildly popular. (Later, when he was confined to a madhouse, it would be one of his occasional delusions that he was a prizefighter, retired because no one was willing to take him on.) It must have been very odd for him in a world in which class was so strongly felt and reflected so visibly in dialect and in dress. He did not write about it much, and in his letters one is given the impression that his policy was to appear to take the new world opened to him in stride. He seems to have returned to Helpston after each visit with a sense of relief.

But he returned to a world without books or painting or

conversations about books and paintings or, what interested him as much or more, the natural world. His poems often remarked upon the heedlessness with which the cowboy and the shepherd, the woodsman and the laborer plodded through fields and woods without seeing anything. If his poems had any design on his readers, it is first of all to make them see, to see what's there, to be adequately amazed by the design of the world, its weathers and colors and its teeming creature life.

It was a world that was changing around him. Almost everyone who has written about his poems has remarked on the impact of the Enclosure Acts on the English countryside. The Industrial Revolution, well under way in those years, had created a ravenous market for sheep's wool. It made grazing land precious, and the great landlords began to enclose what had formerly been The Commons, common land used by villagers to garden and to graze their own animals. Clare describes some of the effects in "The Lamentations of Land Oak Waters":

> *The bawks and eddings are no more,*
> *The pastures too are gone,*
> *The greens, the meadows, and the moors*
> *Are all cut up and done.*
> *There's scarce a greensward spot remains*
> *And scarce a single tree.*
> *All naked are thy native plains.*

Jonathan Bate, Clare's recent biographer, describes the effect in Helpston in the years of Clare's growing up. The new Enclosure laws "enumerated the ownership of every acre, rood, and perch, the position of every road, footway, and public drain. Fences, gates, and No Trespassing signs went up. Trees came down. Streams were stopped in their course so that the line of ditches could be made straight."

When he returned to the village after his first London

adventure, Clare began, not surprisingly, to struggle with depression and the nagging physical ailments that seem to attend it—lingering flus, agues, colds, nameless aches. He was trying to write in a house with ten inhabitants, several of them infants and toddlers, no indoor plumbing, heat in the winter from a fireplace. His fame and the attentions of the local landowners must have separated him from his neighbors. The illnesses were serious enough that his publisher paid for doctor's visits. He liked to drink, and when there was cash in hand, he medicated himself, or cheered himself, with ale. During this time, the critics say, his writing became more his own. The mannerisms of the eighteenth century poets through whom he discovered poetry, their somewhat pedestrian sententiousness, the stock classicisms of "smiling fields" and "wooly tribes," fell away, and his poems became ever more precise, observant, and alive. Childhood became an important theme, childhood as a lost eden, like the lost commons. The disillusionments and struggles of adult life was another theme, and the descriptions in the poems become a self-conscious effort to recover in poetry the innocence of the eye and through it the freshness of the world. He wrote about his project at this time as if it were both a gift and a danger:

> O poesy's power, thou overpowering sweet
> That renders hearts that love thee all unmeet
> For this rude world, its trouble and its care,
> Loading the heart with joys it cannot bear,
> That warms and chills and burns and bursts at last
> O'er broken hopes and troubles never past,
> I pay thee worship at a rustic shrine.

During this time he began to lose his mind. In 1832, an Earl Fitzwilliam, Lord Milton, the grandest of the local landlords, arranged a larger house for the Clare family in the village of Northborough. It was only three miles down the road, and Clare, though he wrote remarkable poems there, found the move wrenching and felt as if he were in exile. He had begun to suffer from intense mood swings and delusions. He was barely able to see his last book through publication in 1835, and in 1837, he was committed to a private asylum for the insane. It seems to have been a quite enlightened institution, run by a sensitive and intelligent doctor who gave Clare free run of the grounds and encouraged him to continue to write poems. (There is a novel about the place, where Tennyson's brother was also an inmate—*The Quickening Maze* by Adam Fould). After three years there, he ran away—he walked the hundred miles back to Northborough and his wife and family, in four desperate days of which he left a vivid account. He was home for five months, during which he continued to behave erratically, and was committed to another institution nearby, the Northampton General Lunatic Asylum, where he lived out his life and continued to write poems for another twenty-two years, all but forgotten by the literary world.

There is something enormously poignant about Clare's mental illness. The tension between his artistic gifts and his social position placed terrific stress on his life, and so did his efforts to sustain a writing life in his physical circumstances. And writing at the level of intensity and concentration he was able to maintain for many years would have been stressful under any circumstances. Any, or all, of this may have contributed to his mental condition and it may simply have been bad luck in brain chemistry. I think there is no way of knowing. But there is something haunting about the form his madness took. One of his recurring delusions was that he was Lord Byron—the iconic poet of the age and one of the wealthiest. Another was that Mary Joyce, his grammar school sweetheart whom he was forbidden to court because he was a peasant and she was a daughter of the middle class, was his second, spiritual wife. He had not seen her since childhood, but wrote a number of very pure and affecting poems to his idea of her. (When he fled the first asylum, he imagined that he was returning to both his wives, only to be told that Mary Joyce, still unmarried, had died several years before in an accidental fire. He simply didn't believe it.) And there was his idea that he was a famous boxer. In a general way, the boundary between what he had experienced personally and experienced in imagination loosened. When he read a book about Wellington, he told visitors anecdotes of soldiering with Wellington. If he read a book about Washington Irving, he described sailing up the Hudson and visiting Irving in Albany. All of this seems like the phantasmal edge of many artists'—many peoples'—mental lives, and it makes Clare's twenty-six years of illness and incarceration particularly rending.

And he continued to write remarkable poems during these years, none of which were published in his lifetime. Here, for example, from 1844—two years into his stay at the second asylum in Northampton—is a sonnet that seems to revisit Keats's "Ode to a Nightingale."

> *This is the month, the Nightingale, clod-brown,*
> *Is heard among the woodland shady boughs.*
> *This is the time when, in the vale, grass-grown,*
> *The maiden hears at eve her lover's vows.*
> *What time the blue mist, round the patient cows,*
> *Dim rises from the grass, and half conceals*
> *Their dappled hides,—I hear the nightingale*
> *That from the little blackthorn spinny steals*
> *To the old hazel hedge that skirts the vale*
> *And still unseen sings sweet:—the ploughman feels*
> *The thrilling music, as he goes along,*
> *And imitates and listens—while the fields*
> *Lose all their paths in dusk, to lead him wrong*
> *Still sings the nightingale her sweet melodious song.*

One of the first pleasures of the poem is that rhyme on "vows" and "cows" and the way the spring mist almost hides their cud-chewing and matter-of-fact existence from the scene. Clare doesn't satirize the clichés of rural wooing, but he teases them. And there is the exact knowledge of that thrush's habitat as "from the little blackthorn spinny" it "steals to the old hazel hedge that skirts the vale." And in case you were not sure he were teasing the lovers, he has the ploughman, caught up by the bird's song—"Thou wast not born for Death, Immortal Bird!" Keats had written—lose his way in the dusk. One might read this as a subtle poem of admonition against being misled by natural desire, natural beauty, but notice that the bird's song is "thrilling" and that he draws out his description of the song in the last line by adding an extra pair of syllables to give it a teasing, over-the-top gorgeousness. This provides the poem its strong and delicate balance—the clod-brown bird and the patient cows. Like many of his later poems it seems to present a scene and withhold comment.

Part of what's singular about Clare is that his birds are entirely birds. In another, earlier poem, "The Nightingale's Nest," he gives us a bird that is anything but immortal. Here is the moment when the speaker—on one of his careless rambles—comes across the bird's nest:

> Aye, as I live, her secret nest is here
> Upon this white thorn stulp—I've searched about
> For hours in vain—there, put that bramble by,
> Nay, trample on its brashes and get near.
> How subtle is the bird. She started out
> And raised a plaintive note of danger night
> Ere we were past the brambles and now near
> Her nest she sudden stops—as choking fear
> That might betray her home. So, even now,
> We'll leave it as we found it—safety's guard
> Of pathless solitude shall keep it still.

In this poem, as in so many others, the creature life is not primarily symbolic, as it is in Keats's great poem—and so many other gorgeous poems in the English tradition. Clare's bird is first of all an animal living its life with its sense of danger and its tactics for survival and its homing place.

In this way it might be said that Keats was among the last of the Miltonic poets and Clare the first of the Darwinian poets. *The Origin of Species* was not published until the last years of Clare's life, but Clare did know the work of Darwin's uncle, Erasmus Darwin, who had published a long botanical poem, and Clare had taken an interest in the new system of classification proposed by Carl Linnaeus. Self-taught, both in literature and science, his mind, when he looked at the world, went straight to empirical observation, to the connectedness of processes and natural events—what had not yet been called ecology—rather than to classical mythology and its rich lore about creatures that had, mostly, to do with human psychology and the forms of human desire. Darwin himself, working on *Origins* in those years went for information to men like Clare—to pigeon breeders and gardeners and amateur ornithologists and naturalists, folks with not much formal education but with fine habits of observation. He had a sense that all forms of organic life were trying to survive and earn a living in the vastly rich and complex network of things he would describe in the last pages of the *Origin* as "a tangled bank."

This is not to say that Clare was uninterested in the inwardness of poetry. Or the poetry of desire. Some of his late poems to the imagined and imaginary Mary Joyce are especially memorable. He had a head full of folk songs, as his father had, and he could transcribe music, as he did listening to the gypsy fiddlers in their encampments around Helpston. His head was also full of the rhythms of the Scots poets Alan Ramsey and Robert Burns. One of his love poems begins

Meet me in the green glen
Beside the tall elm tree
Where the sweet briar smells so sweet agen
There come with me
Meet me in the green glen

Meet me at the sunset
Down in the green glen

> *Where we've often met*
> *By hawthorn tree and fox's den*
> *Meet me in the green glen*

Another, more haunting, is called "Song." Here's the whole of it:

> *I wish I was where I would be*
> *With love alone to dwell.*
> *Was I but her or she but me*
> *Then love would be all well.*
> *I wish to send my thoughts to her*
> *As quick as thought can fly,*
> *But as the winds the waters stir*
> *The mirrors change and fly.*

And for the poetry of self-reflexion there are the late poems, both of which are titled "I Am." One begins:

> *I am, yet what I am, none cares or knows.*
> *My friends forsake me like a memory lost.*
> *I am the self-consumer of my woes.*

So for new readers there is a lot of Clare to get to know. After his death, a biography, not very reliable, appeared. In 1908 the poet Arthur Symons published an edition of his poems that included some of the previously unpublished work. A whole volume of the unpublished work appeared in 1920. Another collection, *Poems of John Clare's Madness* appeared in 1949. Between 1984 and 2003, a team of scholars produced for Oxford University Press a nine volume critical edition of all Clare's poems. It has only been in the last couple of decades that the body of Clare's work was fully available to be absorbed by poets and studied by scholars.

Thus it is not surprising that for many readers Clare will be a new name. It is hard to imagine a better introduction to him than this book of Tom Pohrt's. This is the John Clare, mostly, of his early vigor. This is John Clare out walking. And this book is a gift that allows us to see the world with Clare's amazing eye, to hear it described in the pungent language of his place, and to hear the music of his verse, which, for me, has the self-delight of a gifted artist discovering just how much he could do with his medium. And Tom Pohrt's drawings catch exactly the way the accuracy of a field naturalist and the coloring of affection and imagination are married in Clare's work.

CLARE REPUNCTUATED

My aim was to give twentieth century punctuation to nine-teenth century poems. The punctuation is therefore frugal with commas and semi-colons and it is attentive to sentence rhythm. My ideal was to punctuate Clare as if he were Robert Frost. I found it difficult—particularly in "A Morning Walk"—to be completely consistent. So issues like when to put a comma between two clauses in a compound sentence end up being a subjective judgment based on how close the connection between the clauses is. The task is intuiting Clare's sense of pacing and trying to honor his amazing ear for both iambic lilt and sentence rhythm.

RH

POEMS

Ah sure it is a lovely day
As ever summer's glory yields
And I will put my books away
And wander in the fields

A MORNING WALK

CARELESS RAMBLES

DAY-BREAK

The red east glows. The dewy cheek of day
  Has not yet met the sun's o'erpowering smile.
The dew-drops in their beauty still are gay,
  Save those the shepherd's early steps defile.
  Pleased will I linger o'er the scene awhile —
The black clouds melt away, the larks awaken.
  Sing, rising bird, and I will join with thee.
With day-break's beauties I have much been taken.
  As thy first anthem breath'd its melody,
I've stood and paus'd the varied clouds to see
And warm'd in ecstasy, and look'd and warm'd
  When day's first rays, the far hill top adorning,
Fring'd the blue clouds with gold. O doubly charm'd
  I hung in raptures then on early morning.

Birds' Nests

How fresh the air, the birds how busy now.
In every walk, if I but peep, I find
Nests newly made or finished all and lined
With hair and thistledown, and in the bough
Of a little hawthorn huddled up in green,
The leaves still thickening as the spring gets age,
The pink's quite round and snug and closely laid,
And linnet's of materials loose and rough,
And still hedge-sparrow, moping in the shade
Near the hedge-bottom, weaves of homely stuff—
Dead grass and mosses green—an hermitage
For secrecy and shelter rightly made.
And beautiful it is to walk beside
The lanes and hedges where their homes abide.

PLEASANT SPOTS

There is a wild and beautiful neglect
   About the fields that so delights and cheers,
Where nature her own feelings to effect
   Is left at her own silent work for years,
The simplest thing thrown in our way delights
   From the wild careless feature that it wears.
The very road that wanders out of sight
   Crooked and free is pleasant to behold,
And such the very weeds left free to flower,
   Corn poppies red, and carlock gleaming gold
That makes the corn-field shine in summer's hour
   Like painted skies—and fancy's distant eye
   May well imagine armies marching by
In all the grand array of pomp and power.

CROWS IN SPRING

The crow will tumble up and down
    At the first sight of spring
And in the old trees around the town
    Brush winter from its wing.

No longer flapping far away,
    To naked fen they fly.
Chill fare as on a winter's day,
    But field and valley nigh

Where swains are stirring out to plough
    And woods are just at hand,
They seek the upland's sunny brow
    And strut from land to land

And often flap their sooty wings
    And sturt to neighboring tree
and seem to try all ways to sing
    And almost speak in glee.

The ploughman hears and turns his head
    Above to wonder why,
And there's a new nest nearly made
    Proclaims the winter by.

The schoolboy, free from winter's frown
    That rests on every stile,
In wonder sets his basket down
    To start his happy toil.

The Breath of the Morning

How beautiful and fresh the pastoral smell
  Of tedded hay breathes in the early morn!
Health in these meadows must in summer dwell
  And take her walks among these fields of corn.
I cannot see her, yet her voice is out
  On every breeze that fans my hair about.
Although the sun is scarcely out of bed
  And leans on ground as half awake from sleep,
The boy hath left his mossy-thatched shed
  And bawls right lustily to cows and sheep,
Or, taken with the woodbines overspread,
  Climbs up to pluck them from their thorny bowers,
Half drowned by drops that patter on his head
From leaves bemoistened by night's secret showers.

PLEASANT PLACES

Old ſtone pits, with veined ivy overhung;
Wild, crooked brooks o'er which is rudely flung
A rail and plank that bends beneath the tread;
Old narrow lanes, where trees meet overhead;
Path-ſtiles on which a ſteeple we espy,
Peeping and ſtretching in the diſtant sky;
Heaths overspread with furze-bloom's sunny shine,
Where Wonder pauses to proclaim, "Divine!"
Old ponds, dim-shadowed with a broken tree;—
These are the 'picturesques' of Taſte to me—
While painting winds to make complete the scene
In rich confusion mingle every green,
Waving the sketchy pencils in their hands,
Shading the living scenes to fairy lands.

A Spring Morning

The spring comes in with all her hues and smells,
In freshness breathing over hills and dells,
O'er woods where May her gorgeous drapery flings,
And meads washed fragrant by their laughing springs.
Fresh are new opened flowers, untouched and free
From the bold rifling of the amorous bee.
The happy time of singing birds is come
And love's lone pilgrimage now finds a home.
Among the mossy oaks now coos the dove
And the hoarse crow finds softer notes for love.
The foxes play around their dens and bark
In joy's excess 'mid woodland shadows dark.
The flowers join lips below, the leaves above,
And every sound that meets the ear is love.

BIRDS' NESTS IN THE SPRING

'Tis spring. Warm glows the south,
A chaffinch carries moss in its mouth
To the filbert hedges all day long
And charms the poet with its beautiful song.
The wind blows blea o'er the sedgy fen,
But warm the sun shines by the little wood
Where the old cow at her leisure chews her cud.

The Yellowhammer's Nest

Just by the wooden bridge a bird flew up,
Scared by the cow-boy as he scrambled down
To reach the misty dewberry. Let us stoop
And seek its nest. The brook we need not dread.
'Tis scarcely deep enough a bee to drown
As it sings harmless o'er its pebbly bed.
Aye, here it is! Stuck close beside the bank
Beneath the bunch of grass that spindles rank
Its husk-seeds tall and high. 'Tis rudely planned
Of bleached stubbles and the withered fare
That last year's harvest left upon the land,
Lined thinly with the horse's sable hair.
Five eggs, pen-scribbled o'er with ink their shells,
Resembling writing scrawls which fancy reads
As nature's posey and pastoral spells—
They are the yellowhammer's, and she dwells,
Most poet-like, where brooks and flowery weeds
As sweet as Castaly her fancy deems,
And that old mole-hill is Parnassus' hill
On which her partner happily sits and dreams
O'er all his joys of song. Let's leave it still
A happy home of sunshine, flowers, and streams.
Yet is the sweetest place exposed to ill,
A noisome weed that burdens every soil,
For snakes are known with chill and deadly coil
To watch such nests and seize the helpless young,
And, like as if the plague becomes a guest,
To leave a houseless home, a ruined nest.
Aye! Mournful hath the little warbler sung
When such-like woes have rent his gentle breast.

HEDGE-SPARROW

The tame hedge-sparrow in its russet dress
Is half a robin for its gentle ways,
And the bird-loving dame can do no less
Than throw it out a crumb on cold days.
In early March it into gardens ſtrays
And in the snug clipt box-tree green and round
It makes a neſt of moss and hair and lays
Its eggs in number five of greenish blue,
Bright, beautiful, and glossy shining shells
Much like the firetail's but of brighter hue.
Yet in her garden home much danger dwells
Where skulking cat with mischief in its breaſt
Catches their young before they leave the neſt.

THE NIGHTINGALE'S NEST

Up this green woodland-ride let's softly rove
And liſt the nightingale — she dwells juſt here.
Hush! Let the wood gate softly clap, for fear
The noise might drive her from her home of love,
For here I've learned her many a merry year,
At morn, at eve, nay, all the live-long day,
As though she lived on song. This very spot,
Juſt where the old-man's beard all wildly trails
Rude arbors o'er the road and tops the way,
And where that child its blue-bell flowers hath got,
Laughing and creeping through the mossy rails,
There have I hunted like a very boy,
Creeping on hands and knees through matted thorn
To find her neſt and see her feed her young.
And vainly did I many hours employ:
All seemed as hidden as a thought unborn,
And where those crimping fern-leaves ramp among
The hazel's under boughs, I've neſtled down
And watched her while she sung, and her renown
Hath made me marvel that so famed a bird
Should have no better dress than russet brown.
Her wings would tremble in her ecſtasy
And feathers ſtand on end, as 'twere with joy,
And mouth wide open to release her heart
Of its out-sobbing songs. The happieſt part
Of summer's fame she shared, for so to me
Did happy fancies shapen her employ,
But if I touched a bush or scarcely ſtirred,
All in a moment ſtopt. I watched in vain.
The timid bird had left the hazel bush
And at a diſtance hid to sing again.
Loſt in a wilderness of liſtening leaves,
Rich ecſtasy would pour its luscious ſtrain,
Till envy spurred the emulating thrush

To start less wild and scarce inferior songs,
For while of half the year care him bereaves
To damp the ardor of his speckled breast,
The nightingale to summer's life belongs,
And naked trees and winter's nipping wrongs
Are strangers to her music and her rest.
Her joys are evergreen, her world is wide.
Hark! There she is as usual—let's be hush—
For in this black-thorn clump, if rightly guessed,
Her curious house is hidden. Part aside
These hazel branches in a gentle way
And stoop right cautious 'neath the rustling boughs,

For we will have another search today
And hunt this fern-strewn thorn-clump round and round,
And where this reeded wood-grass idly bows,
We'll wade right through. It is a likely nook.
In such-like spots, and often on the ground,
They'll build, where rude boys never think to look.
Aye, as I live! Her secret nest is here
Upon this white-thorn stump! I've searched about
For hours in vain. There! Put that bramble by—
Nay, trample on its branches and get near.
How subtle is the bird! She started out
And raised a plaintive note of danger nigh
Ere we were past the brambles, and now, near
Her nest, she sudden stops, as choking fear
That might betray her home. So even now

We'll leave it as we found it. Safety's guard
Of pathless solitudes shall keep it still.
See there! She's sitting on the old oak bough,
Mute in her fears. Our presence doth retard
Her joys, and doubt turns every rapture chill.
Sing on, sweet bird! May no worse hap befall
Thy visions than the fear that now deceives.
We will not plunder music of its dower,
Nor turn the spot of happiness to thrall,
For melody seems hid in every flower
That blossoms near thy home. These harebells all
Seem bowing with the beautiful song,
And gaping cuckoo-flower with spotted leaves
Seems blushing of the singing it has heard.
How curious is the nest. No other bird
Uses these loose materials or weaves
Its dwelling in such spots — dead oaken leaves
Are placed without, and velvet moss within,
And little scraps of grass, and, scant and spare,
What scarcely seems materials, down and hair,
For from men's haunts she nothing seems to win.
Yet Nature is the builder and contrives
Homes for her children's comfort even here,
Where solitude's disciples spend their lives
Unseen, save when a wanderer passes near
That loves such pleasant places. Deep adown,
The nest is made a hermit's mossy cell.
Snug lie her curious eggs in number five,
Of deadened green, or rather olive brown,
And the old prickly thorn-bush guards them well.
So here we'll leave them, still unknown to wrong,
As the old woodland's legacy of song.

CARELESS RAMBLES

I love to wander at my idle will
   In summer's luscious prime about the fields,
To kneel, when thirsty, at the little rill
   And sip the draught its pebbly bottom yields,
And where the maple bush its fountain shields
   To lie and rest a sultry hour away,
Cropping the swelling peascod from the land,
   Or mid the sheltering woodland-walks to stray
Where oaks for aye o'er their old shadows stand,
'Neath whose dark foliage with a welcome hand
   I pluck the luscious strawberry, ripe and red
As Beauty's lips — and in my fancy's dreams,
   As 'mid the velvet moss I mussing tread,
Feel life as lovely as her picture seems.

The Daisy

The daisy is a happy flower
    And comes at early spring
And brings with it the sunny hour
    When bees are on the wing.

It brings with it the butterfly
    And humble early bee
With the polyanthus' golden eye
    And blooming apple tree.

Hedge sparrows form the mossy nest
    In the old garden hedge
Where schoolboys in their idle glee
    Seek pooties as their pledge.

The cow stands blooming all the day
    Over the orchard gate
And eats her bits of sweet mown hay
    And Goody stands to wait.

Lest what's not eaten the rude wind
    May rise and snatch away
Over the neighbor's hedge behind
    Where hungry cattle lay.

A Morning Walk

Ah sure it is a lovely day
As ever summer's glory yields
And I will put my books away
And wander in the fields.
Just risen is the red round sun,
Cock from the roost doth loudly brawl
And house bee busily begun
Hums round the mortared wall,

And while I take my staff to start,
Birds sing among the eldern leaves
And fighting sparrows, glad at heart,
Chirp in the cottage eaves,
Nor can I help but turn and view,
Ere yet I close the creaking door,
The sunbeams eager peeping through
Upon the sanded floor.

The twilight streak of lightsome grey
Hath from the eastern summit gone
And clouds clothed in the pride of day
Put golden liveries on.
The creeping sun, large, round and red,
Yet higher hastens up and higher
Till blazing o'er its cloudy bed
It shines a ball of fire.

Cows now their morning meals pursue,
The carthorse to its labor's sped,
And sheep shake off the nightly dew
Just risen from their bed.
The maids are out and many a smile
Are left them by the passing swain
Who, as they lightly skip the stile,
Will turn and smile again.

All nightly things are on the run,
By daylight's burning smiles betrayed,
And gnats retreating from the sun
Fly dancing to the shade.
The snail is stealing from the light
Where grass a welcome shelter weaves,
And white moths shrink in cool delight
Behind the bowering leaves.

The hares their fearful morsels eat
Till by a snuffling dog descried,
Then, hastening to their snug retreat,
They waited eventide.
The rabbit bustled out of sight
Nor longer cropt each thymy hill,
But seeks his den where gloomy night
Is kept imprisoned still.

The walks that sweetest pleasure yields
When things appear so fresh and fair
Are when we wander round the fields
To breathe the morning air.
The fields like spring seem young, and gay
The dewy trees and painted sky,
And larks as sweetly as in May
Still whistle as they fly.

The woods that oft my step receives
I cannot search for resting bowers,
For when I touch the sleepy leaves
Dew patters down in showers,
But I can range the green and share
The charms the pasture scene displays,
Crooking down sheep tracks here and there
That lead a thousand ways.

Bowing, dewdropping by the stream,
The flowers glow lively on the sight
Awaking from night's summer dream
As conscious of delight,
Nor could I crop them in such hours
Without regret that I'd destroyed
A joy in my companion flowers
As sweet as I enjoyed.

The stinking finweed's blushing bloom—
Their pea-like flowers appear so fair
That bees will to their bosoms come
And hope for honey there,
For bumble bees ere flowers are dry
Will wake and brush the trembling dew
And drone as melancholy by
When dreams are proved untrue.

While winding rushbeds winding through
I idly swing my staff about
To free their tasseled tops from dew.
The leveret startles out,
And now the lark starts from its nest
But not to sing—on thistle nigh
It perks in fear and prunes its breast
Till I have journeyed by.

The resting cow just turns its head
To stare, then chews its cud again.
The colt more timid leaves its bed
And shakes its shaggy mane.
The shoy sheep fly and faster still,
The wet grass smoking 'neath their flight,
When shepherds urged their whistles shrill
And dogs appear in sight.

Still there is joy that will not cease,
Calm hovering o'er the face of things,
That sweet tranquility and peace
That morning ever brings.
The shadows by the sun portrayed
Lie basking in the golden light.
E'en little hillocks stretch their shade
As if they loved the sight.

The brook seemed purling sweeter by
As freshened from the cooling light
And on its breaſt the morning sky
Smiles beautiful and bright.
The pool's ſtill depth as night was by
Warmed as to life in curling rings,
Stirred by the touch of water fly
Or zephyr's gentle wings.

And cows did on its margin lie
As bleſt as morn did never cease
And knapping horses grazed slowly by
That added to is peace.
No flies diſturbed the herding boys
Save flies the summer water breeds
That harmless shared the morning's joys
And hummed among the weeds.

Birds fluttered round the water's brink,
Then perched their dabbled wings to dry
And swallows often ſtooped to drink
And twittered gladly by
And on the brook-bank's rushy ridge
Larks sat the morning sun to share
And doves where ivy hides the bridge
Sing soothing ditties there.

The leaves of ash and elms and willows
That skirt the paſture's wildered way
Heaved to the breeze in gentle billows
Of mingled green and grey.
The birds, the breeze, the milker's call,
The brook that in the sun did gliſten
Told morn's delight that smiled on all
As one that loves to liſten.

O who can shun the lovely morning,
The calms, the crowds of beauteous things?
O where's the soul that treats with scorning
The beauty morning brings
With dew-drops braided round her hair
And opening flowers her breaſt adorning?
O where's the soul that cannot share
The loveliness of morning?

By hedgerow side and field and brook
I love to be its partner ſtill,
To turn each leaf of nature's book
Where all may read as will
And he who loves it not deſtroys
His quiet and makes life a slave.
His soul is dead to loves and joys,
His own heart is their grave.

The very boys appear to share
The joy of morning's lovely hours,
In rapture running here and there
To ſtick their hats with flowers.
Some loll them by a reſting ſtile
To liſten pleasing things around—
Dove, lark and bee—and try the while
To imitate the sound.

The shepherd muses o'er his hook
And quiet as the morning seems
Or reads some, wild myſterious book
On 'fortunes, moles and dreams,'
While by his side as bleſt as he
His dog in peaceful slumber lies,
Unwakened as he used to be
To watch the teasing flies.

Rapt in delight I long have stood
Gazing on scenes that seem to smile
And now to view far field and wood
I climb this battered stile.
There sails the paddock still and proud,
Assailed at first by swopping crows
But soon it meets the morning cloud
And scorns such humble foes.

The mist that round the distance bent
By woodland side and sloping hill
Fled as each minute came and went
More far and farther still,
And the blue ridge which night renewed
Round the horizon's fairy way
More faster than the eye pursued
Shrank unperceived away.

By leaning trees beneath the swail
For pleasing things I love to look
Or loll o'er oak bridge's guarding rail
That ſtrideth o'er the brook
To mark the willow row,
The painted windmill's peeping sails,
Seeming in its journey slow
Pleased with the easy, gentle gales.

And oft I sit me on the ground
Musing upon a neighboring flower
Or liſt' the church-clock's humming sound
To count the passing hour
Or mark the brook its journey take
In gentle curves round many a weed
Or hear the soft wind awake
Among the ruſtling reed.

Fragment

The elm tree's heavy foliage meets the eye
Propt in dark masses on the evening sky.
The lighter ash but half obstructs the view,
Leaving grey openings where the light looks through.

The Hollow Tree

How oft a summer shower has started me
To seek the shelter of a hollow tree:
Old huge ash-dotterel wasted to a shell
Whose vigorous head still grew and flourished well,
Where ten might sit upon the battered floor
And still look round discovering room for more,
And he who chooses a hermit life to share
Might have a door and make a cabin there.
They seemed so like a house that our desires
Would call them so and make our gypsy fires
And eat field dinners of the juicy peas
Till we were wet and drabbled to the knees.
But in our old tree-house, rain as it might,
Not one drop fell although it rained till night.

Flow on Winding River

Flow on, winding river, in silence forever.
The sedge and flags rustle about in a bustle.
You are dear to my fancy, thou smooth flowing river.
The bulrush bows calm and there's peace in the hustle
      As the boat gently glides
      O'er thy soft flowing tides
As the young maidens sail on a sweet summer day.

The wavelets in ridges by osiers through bridges
'Neath the grey willow shade and the nestling reeds made
Were dear to my fancy as onward they sail.
The osiers they dip in the rings lilies made
      And the maiden look'd red
      As the corn poppy bed
Or dog rose that blushed in the shade.

The day was delightful where but gadflies were spiteful.
The hum of the bee caroled merrily there.
The butterflies danced round the wild flowers delightful
And the old willows too's their grey locks in the air.
      The boat softly rippled,
      Suspended oars drippled
While the maidens were lovely and beauteously fair.

The boat gently pushes aside the bulrushes
All gilt by the water and summer sunbeams.
How soft the oar dashes the ſtream as it splashes
By the side of the boat with its burden of dreams.
      The rushing of waters,
      The songs of earth's daughters,
How sweetly they sound in the plash of the ſtreams.

An Idle Hour

Sauntering at ease, I often love to lean
  O'er old bridge walls and mark the flood below—
Whose ripples through the weeds of oily green,
  Like happy travelers, chatter as they go—
And view the sunshine dancing on the arch,
  Time keeping to the merry waves beneath,
While on the banks some drooping blossoms parch,
  Thirsting for water in the day's hot breath,
Right glad of mud-drops splashed upon their leaves
  By cattle plunging from the steepy brink.
Each water-flower more than its share receives
  And revels to its very cups in drink.
So, in the world, some strive and fare but ill
While others riot and have plenty still.

The Happy Bird

The happy white-throat on the swaying bough,
  Rocked by the impulse of the gadding wind
That ushers in the April showers, now
  Carols right joyously, and now reclined,
Crouching, she clings to her moving seat
  To keep her hold, and till the wind for rest
Pauses, she mutters inward melodies
  That seem her heart's rich thinkings to repeat,
But when the branch is still, her little breast
  Swells out in rapture's gushing symphonies,
And then, against her brown wing softly pressed,
  The wind comes playing, an enraptured guest.
This way and that she swings, till gusts arise
More boisterous in their play. Then off she flies.

Burthorp Oak

Old noted oak! I saw thee in a mood
  Of vague indifference, and yet with me
Thy memory, like thy fate, hath lingering stood
  For years, thou hermit in the lonely sea
Of grass that waves around thee! Solitude
  Paints not a lonelier picture to the view,
Burthorp! Than thy one melancholy tree,
  Age-rent, and shattered to a stump. Yet new
Leaves come upon each rift and broken limb
  With every spring, and Poesy's visions swim
Around it of old days and chivalry,
  And desolate fancies bid the eyes grow dim
With feelings, that earth's grandeur should decay
  And all its olden memories pass away.

Evening Primrose

When once the sun sinks in the weſt
And dew-drops pearl the evening's breaſt,
Almoſt as pale as moonbeams are
Or its companionable ſtar,
The evening primrose opes anew
Its delicate blossoms to the dew
And hermit-like, shunning the light,
Waſtes its fair bloom upon the night
Who, blindfold to the fond caresses,
Knows not the beauty he possesses.
Thus it blooms on with night is by.
When day looks out with open eye,
'Bashed at the gaze it cannot shun,
It faints and withers and is gone.

The Droning Bee

1.

The droning bee has wakened up
And hums around the buttercup
And round the bright ſtar-daisy hums.
 O'er every blade of grass he passes,
The dew-drop shines like looking glasses.
 In every drop a bright sun comes.
'Tis March, and spring, bright days we see.
 Round every blossom hums the bee.

2.

As soon as daylight in the morning,
 The crimson curtain of the dawning,
We hear, and see, the humming bee
 Searching for hedge row violets,
 Happy with the food he gets,
Swimming o'er brook and meadow lea;
 Then sits on maple ſtools at reſt,
 On the green mosses' velvet breaſt.

3.

About the molehill, round and round,
 The wild bee hums with honeyed sound,
Singing a song of spring and flowers
 To schoolboys heard in sunny hours
 When all the waters seem a blaze
Of fire and sunshine in such days
 When bees buzz on with coal black eye,
 Joined by the yellow butterfly.

4.

And when it comes, a summer shower,
 It ſtill will go from flower to flower.
Then underneath the rushes
 It sees the silver daisy flower
 And there it spends a little hour,
Then hides among the bushes.
 But whence they come from, where they go,
 None but the wiser schoolboys know.

THE ETERNITY OF NATURE

Leaves, from eternity, are simple things
To the world's gaze—whereto a spirit clings
Sublime and lasting. Trampled under foot,
The daisy lives and strikes its little root
Into the lap of time. Centuries may come
And pass away into the silent tomb
And still the child hid in the womb of time
Shall smile and pluck them, when this simple rhyme
Shall be forgotten like a churchyard stone,
Or lingering lie unnoticed and alone.
When eighteen hundred years, our common date,
Grow many thousands in their marching state,
Aye, still the child with pleasure in his eye
Shall cry—the daisy! a familiar cry,
And run to pluck it in the self-same state
As when time found it in his infant date
And, like a child himself, when all was new,
Might smile with wonder and take notice too.
Its little golden bosom frilled with snow
Might win e'en Eve to stoop adown and show
Her partner Adam in the silky grass
This little gem that smiled where pleasure was
And, loving Eve, from Eden followed ill
And bloomed with sorrow and lives smiling still.
As once in Eden under heaven's breath,
So now on earth and on the lap of death
It smiles forever. Cowslips' golden blooms
That in the closen and the meadow come
Shall come when kings and empires fade and die,
And in the meadows as time's partners lie
As fresh two thousand years to come as now,
With those five crimson spots upon their brow.
The little brooks that hum a simple lay
In green unnoticed spots, from praise away,

Shall sing when poets in time's darkness hid
Shall lie like memory in a pyramid
Forgetting yet not all forgot, though lost
Like a thread's end in raveled windings crossed.
The little humble-bee shall hum as long
As nightingales, for time protects the song
And nature is their soul to whom all clings
Of fair and beautiful in lasting things.
The little robin in the quiet glen,
Hidden from fame and all the strife of men,
Sings unto time a pastoral and gives
A music that lives on and ever lives.
Spring and autumnal years shall bloom and fade,
Longer than songs that poets ever made.
Think ye not these, time's playthings, pass proud skill?
Time loves them like a child and ever will,
And so I worship them in bushy spots
And sing with them when all else notice not,
And feel the music of their mirth agree
With that sooth quiet that bestirs in me.
And if I touch aright that quiet tone,
That soothing truth that shadows forth their own,
Then many a year shall grow in after days
And still find hearts to love my quiet lays.
Yet cheering mirth with thoughts sung not for fame
But for the joy that with their utterance came,
That inward breath of rapture urged not loud—
Birds, singing lone, fly silent past a crowd—
So in these pastoral spots which childish time
Makes dear to me, I wander out and rhyme
What hour the dewy morning's infancy
Hangs on each blade of grass and every tree,
And sprents the red thighs of the bumble bee
Who 'gins betimes unwearied minstrelsy,
Who breakfasts, dines, and most divinely sups
With every flower save golden buttercups

on whose proud bosoms he will never go
And passes by with scarcely "how do ye do,"
Since in their showy, shining, gaudy cells
May be the summer's honey never dwells.
Her ways are mysteries all! Yet endless youth
Lives in them all, unchangeable as truth.
With the odd number five, strange nature's laws
Play many freaks, nor once mistake the cause,
For in the cowslip-pips this very day
Five spots appear, which time wears not away
Nor once mistakes the counting—look within
Each pip, and five, nor more nor less, is seen,
And trailing bindweed with its pinky cup
Five leaves of paler hue go streaking up,
And birds a many keep the rule alive,
Laying five eggs, nor more nor less than five.
And flowers, how many own that mystic power
With five leaves ever making up the flower!
The five-leaved grass, mantling its golden cup
Of flowers—five leaves make all for which I stoop,
And briony in the hedge that now adorns
The tree to which it clings, and now the thorns,
Owns five-starred point leaves of dingy white.
Count which I will, all make the number right.
The spreading goose-grass, trailing all abroad
In leaves of silver green about the road—
Five leaves make every blossom all along.
I stoop for many, none are counted wrong.
'Tis nature's wonder and her maker's will
who bade earth be and order owns him still
as that superior power who keeps the key
of wisdom, power, and might through all eternity.

LITTLE TROTTY WAGTAIL

1.

Little trotty wagtail he went in the rain
And tittering tottering sideways he ne'er got ſtraight again.
He ſtooped to get a worm and looked up to catch a fly
And then he flew away ere his feathers they were dry.

2.

Little trotty wagtail he waddled in the mud
And left his little foot marks trample where he would.
He waddled in the water-pudge and waggle went his tail
And chirrup up his wings to dry upon the garden rail.

3.

Little trotty wagtail you nimble all about
And in the dimpling water-pudge you waddle in and out.
Your home is night at hand and in the warm pigſty
So little Maſter Wagtail I'll bid you a "Good bye."

Rural Scenes

I never saw a man in all my days,
  One whom the calm of quietness pervades,
Who gave not woods and fields his heart praise
  And felt a happiness in summer shades.
There I meet common thoughts that all may read
  Who love the quiet fields. I note them well
Because they give me joy as I proceed
  And joy renewed when I their beauties tell
In simple verse and unambitious songs
  That in some mossy cottage haply may
Be read, and win the praise of humble tongues
  In the green shadows of some after-day.
For rural fame may likeliest rapture yield
To hearts whose songs are gathered from the fields.

The Shepherd's Tree

Huge elm! With rifted trunk all notched and scarred
  Like to a warrior's destiny, I love
To stretch me often on thy shadowed sward
  And hear the laugh of summer leaves above
Or on thy buttressed roots to sit and lean
  In careless attitude and there reflect
On times and deeds and darings that have been,
  Old castaways now swallowed in neglect,
While thou are towering in thy strength of heart,
  Stirring the soul to vain imaginings
In which life's sordid being hath no part.
  The wind of that eternal ditty sings
Humming of future things that burn the mind
To leave some fragment of itself behind.

SUMMER

How sweet, when weary, dropping on a bank.
　Turning a look around on things that be—
E'en feather-headed grasses, spindling, rank,
　A trembling to the breeze one loves to see,
　And yellow buttercup where many a bee
Comes buzzing to its head and bows it down,
　And the great dragonfly with gauzy wings
In gilded coat of purple, green, or brown,
　That on broad leaves of hazel basking clings,
　Fond of the sunny day,—and other things
Past counting please me while thus here I lie.
　But still reflective pains are not forgot.
Summer sometime shall bless this spot, when I
　Hapt in the cold, dark grave can heed it not.

The Ants

What wonder ſtrikes the curious while he views
  The black ant's city by a rotten tree
Or woodland bank. In ignorance we muse,
  Pausing, annoy'd. We know not what we see,
  Such government and thought there seem to be,
Some looking on and urging some to toil,
  Dragging their loads of bent-ſtalks slavishly,
And what's more wonderful, when big loads foil
  One ant or two to carry, quickly then
A swarm flock round to help their fellow-men.
  Surely they speak a language whisperingly
Too fine for us to hear, and sure their ways
  Prove they have kings and laws, and that they be
Deformed remnants of the Fairy-days.

To a Red Clover Blossom

Sweet bottle-shaped flower of lushy red,
  Born when the summer wakes her warmeſt breeze,
Among the meadow's waving grasses spread
  Or 'neath the shade of hedge or clumping trees,
Bowing on slender ſtem thy heavy head,
  In sweet delight I view thy summer bed
And liſt the drone of heavy humble-bees
  Along thy honey'd garden gaily led
Down corn-fields, ſtriped balks, and paſture leas.
  Fond warmings of the soul that long have fled
Revive my bosom with their kindlings ſtill
  As I bend musing o'er thy ruddy pride,
Recalling days when, dropt upon a hill,
  I cut my oaten trumpets by thy side.

THE MOUSE'S NEST

I found a ball of grass among the hay
And progged it as I passed and went away,
And when I looked I fancied something ſtirred
And turned again and hoped to catch a bird,
When out an old mouse bolted in the wheat
With all her young ones hanging at her teats.
She looked so odd and so grotesque to me,
I ran and wondered what the thing could be
And pushed the knapweed bunches where I ſtood.
When the mouse hurried from the craking brood,
The young ones squeaked, and when I went away,
She found her neſt again among the hay.
The water o'er the pebbles scarce could run
And broad old cesspools glittered in the sun.

A Woodland Seat

Within this pleasant wood beside the lane
  Let's sit and rest us from the burning sun
And hide us in the leaves and entertain
  An hour away to watch the wood-brook run
Through heaps of leaves, drop dribbling after drop,
  Pining for freedom till it climbs along
In eddying fury o'er the foamy top
  And then loud laughing sings its whimpling song,
Kissing the misty dewberry by its side
  With eager salutations and in joy,
Making the flag-leaves dance in graceful pride,
  Giving and finding joy. Here we employ
An hour right profitably, thus to see
  Life may meet joys where few intruders be.

Observe the flowers around us, how they live
  Not only for themselves, as we may feel,
But for the joy which they to others give,
  For nature never will her gifts conceal
From those who love to seek them. Here amid
  These trees how many blooms disclose their pride,
From the unthinking rustic only hid
  Who never turns him from the road aside
To look for beauties which he values not.
  It gives one greater zest to feel the joy
We meet in this sweet solemn-suited spot
  And with high ecstasy one's mind employ
To bear the worst that fickle life prepares,
  Finding her sweets are common as her cares.

In every trifle something lives to please
    Or to instruct us. Every weed and flower
Heirs beauty as a birth-right, by degrees
    Of more or less, though taste alone hath power
To see and value what the rest pass by.
    This common dandelion—mark how fine
Its hue. The shadow of the day's proud eye
    Glows not more rich of gold. That nettle there,
Trod down by rustics every hour—
    Search but its slighted blooms. Kings cannot wear
Robes prankt with half the splendor of a flower
    Penciled with hues of workmanship divine,
Bestowed to simple things, denied to power,
    And sent to gladden hearts as low as mine.

Insects

These tiny loiterers on the barley's beard
And happy units of a numerous herd
Of playfellows the laughing summer brings,
Mocking the sunshine on their glittering wings,
How merrily they creep and run and fly!
No kin they bear to labor's drudgery,
Smoothing the velvet of the pale hedge-rose.
And where they fly to dinner no one knows.
The dew-drops feed them not. They love the shine
Of noon whose suns may bring them golden wine.
All day they're playing in their Sunday dress.
Till night goes sleep and they can do no less.
Then to the heath-bell's purple hood they fly
And like to princes in their slumber lie,
Secure from rain and dropping dews and all
In silken beds and roomy painted hall.
So happily they spend their summer day,
Now in the corn-fields, now the new-mown hay,
One almost fancies that such happy things
In colored hoods and richly burnished wings
Are fairy folk in splendid masquerade,
Disguised through fear of mortal folk, afraid,
Keeping their merry pranks a mystery still,
Lest glaring day should do their secrets ill.

To the Fox Fern

Haunter of woods, lone wilds and solitudes
Where none but feet of birds and things as wild
Do print a foot track near, where summer's light,
Buried in boughs, forgets its glare and round thy crimped leaves
Feints in a quiet dimness fit for musings
And melancholy moods, with here and there
A golden thread of sunshine stealing through
The evening-shadowy leaves that seem to creep
Like leisure in the shade.

Pleasures of Fancy

A path, old tree, goes by thee, crooking on,
And through this little gate that claps and bangs
Against thy rifted trunk what steps have gone!
Though but a lonely way, yet mystery hangs
O'er crowds of pastoral scenes recordless here.
The boy might climb the nest in thy young boughs
That's slept half an eternity. In fear
The herdsman may have left his startled cows
For shelter when heaven's thunder voice was near.
Here too the woodman on his wallet laid
For pillow may have slept an hour away,
And poet pastoral, lover of the shade,
Here sat and mused half some long summer day
While some old shepherd listened to the lay.

The Water Lilies on the Meadow Stream

The water lilies on the meadow stream
    Again spread out their leaves of glossy green;
And some, yet young, of a rich copper gleam,
    Scarce open, in the sunny stream are seen,
Throwing a richness upon Leisure's eye,
    That thither wanders in a vacant joy;
While on the sloping banks, luxuriantly,
    Tending of horse and cow, the chubby boy,
In self-delighted whims, will often throw
    Pebbles, to hit and splash their sunny leaves;
Yet quickly dry again, they shine and glow
    Like some rich vision that his eye deceives;
Spreading above the water, day by day,
In dangerous deeps, yet out of danger's way.

The Water Lilies

The water lilies' white and yellow flowers,
  How beautiful they are upon the lake!
I've stood and looked upon the place for hours
  And thought how fine a garden they would make.
The pleasant leaves upon the water float.
  The dragon-fly would come and stay for hours
And, when the water pushed the pleasure boat,
  Would find a safer place among the flowers.
They lay like pleasure in a quiet place,
  Close where the moor-hen loved her nest to make.
They lay like beauty with a smiling face,
  And I have called them 'ladies of the lake,'
I've brought the longest pole and stood for hours,
And tried for years before I got those flowers!

The Milking Shed

Good heaven! And can it be that such a nook
  As this can raise such sudden rapture up?
  Two dottrel trees, an oak and ash, that ſtoop
Their aged bodies o'er a little brook
  And raise their sheltering heads above and o'er
A little hovel raised on four old props
  Old as themselves to look on—and what more?
Nought but a hawthorn hedge, and yet one ſtops
  In admiration and in joy to gaze
Upon these objects, feeling, as I ſtand,
  That nought in all this wide world's thorny ways
Can match this bit of feeling's fairy land.
  How can it be? Time owns the potent spell.
I've known it from a boy and love it well.

Sunset

Welcome, sweet eve! Thy gently sloping sky
  And softly whispering wind that breathes of rest
And clouds unlike what daylight galloped by,
  Now stopt and weary, huddling in the west,
Each by the farewell of day's closing eye
  Left with the smiles of heaven on its breast.
Meek nurse of weariness! How sweet to meet
  Thy soothing tenderness to none denied,
To hear thy whispering voice—ah, heavenly sweet,
  Musing and listening by thy gentle side,
Lost to life's cares, thy colored skies to view,
  Picturing of pleasant worlds unknown to care,
And when our bark the rough sea flounders through,
  Warming in hopes its end shall harbor there.

The Holiday Walk

Come, Eliza and Anna, lay by top and ball
And, friendly boy, throw away cart and toys all,
   Look about for your hats and dispense with your play,
   We'll seek for the fields and be happy today.
Do but hark at the shouts of the boys by the school
As noisy and merry as geese in a pool,
   While the Master himself is so sick of his thrall
   That he laughs like the merriest child of them all.
While they race with their shadows, he joins in the play
And leaps o'er the 'cat gallows' as nimble as they,
   As glad to get out of his school in the sun
   As a captive would be from a prison to run.
The morning invites us to walk. Come along.
'Tis so sweet that the sparrow e'en tries at a song.
   The dews are all gone save among the deep glooms
   'Neath the wood's crowded leaves where the sun never comes,
Nor need we regret that the dews linger there,
For brambles defy us to come if we dare,
   And doubtless each poor little bird in the end
   Is glad to consider the bramble its friend,
For girls even often its dwelling destroys
And boys are so cruel, birds cannot like boys.
   So we'll be contented to roam far away
   Through beanfields in blossom and closes of hay.
Do but look at those ducks, how delighted they seem,
All plashing and cleaning themselves in the stream
   And the swallow that loves in black chimneys to sing
   Will scarcely dart o'er without washing his wing.
Now we're out of the town — see the fields, how they smile
So sweet that the boy climbs astride on the stile
   To gaze round about him as much as to say
   'I should like to go where it pleased me today,'
But poor little fellow, he wishes in spite
Of his toil, for his sheep they want tending till night.

Look here as we come in this cool narrow lane
How close martins pass us and pass us again.
Darting on by the side of the hedges they go
As swift as an arrow shot out of a bow.
  The dust is all past which we met in the street
  And the grass like a carpet spreads under our feet.
See, there's a fine butterfly sits on a leaf.
Aye, you may go creeping as still as a thief,
  It can hear you and see you—see there! up it flies
  With wings like the rainbow you've seen in the skies.
Yes, yes, you may run—there it crosses the stream
As far out of reach as the joy in a dream.
  Aye, now it delights ye to look at the sky.
  Those are hawks sailing proud as the clouds and as high.
See, there one's at rest hanging still even now,
As fixed in the air as a bird on a bough.
  These are sweet sights in sooth, but the milking maid sees
  The sky every morning near sweeter than these
When she hies to her cows while the sun, large and round,
Starts up like a table of fire from the ground
  And she sees it so often she gives it no praise,
  Though some never saw it, not once in their days.
This morning I marked in what splendor he rose,
Like a king in the east ere his journey he goes.
  His bed in the skies any fancy might trace
  With a curtain of scarlet half hiding her face.
Then as he rose up to his throne for a seat,
It changed to a carpet of gold at his feet.
  Then, as a magician's wand touched it, there came
  A dye o'er the east of all hues ye can name,
A dappled profusion of gold, blue and red
Like pavements of rubies where angels have tread.
  A shadow e'en now of its splendor remains
  Like an old ruined tapestry, all blotches and stains,
Giving lessons of grandeur and earthly parade—
To think even heaven hath glories that fade.

Nay, sigh not at all, you shall see by and by
The sunrise as oft as the milkmaid and I.
Stop! There's a wasps' nest, what a bustle and hum
Like legions of armies where danger is come.
  There they rush one by one in their jackets of yellow,
  Not one offers fight, but he's backed by his fellow,
So come on not search at that rose on the bower.
We'll hazard no wounds for the sake of a flower.
  Here's the snail with his fine painted shell at his back,
And there's one without in his jacket of black.
The path's even covered with insects — each sort
  Flock by, crowds in the smiles of the morning to sport:
  There's the cricket in brown and his cousin in green,
  The grasshopper dancing, and o'er them is seen
The ladybird dressed like a hunter in red,

Creeping out from the blossom with whom she went bed.
  So good little girls, now disturb not their play
  And you, Freddy, stop till they hop far away,
For to kill them in sport, as many folks will,
And call it a pastime 'tis cruel and ill,
  As their lives are as sweet of enjoyment as ours
  And they dote like yourselves upon sunshine and flowers.
See yonder's some boys all at swee in the cool
On the wood-riding gate playing truant from school,
  How gladly they seek the field's freedom to play,
  To swee creaking gates and to roll in the hay.
Mocking loud, the wood echoes that answer again
In musical 'haloos' so soft and so plain

That they no longer dread them as giants or elves
But think them all boys fond of sports as themselves
And they shout in their pastimes to coax them away
From the woods' gloomy arbors to join in their play.
　Now, loves, ye are weary I see by your walk.
　Well, well, here's a sweet cock of hay on the baulk.
An ash hung with ivy too leans from the stile,
So sit you down here and we'll rest us awhile,
　But not on that molehill, for see what a mass
　Of pismires are nimbling about in the grass.
If you had crumbs to throw them, they'd haul them away
And never seem weary the whole summer's day,
　And if you sit on them, as small as they are,
　They'll sting you and tease you, so prithee beware!
Do but look how the fields slope away from our eyes
Till the trees in the distance seem clouds in the skies.
　A map spreads about us in green of all stains,
　Dark woods, paler meadows, and fields' varied grains,
And look o'er the gap of yon hedge and behold
Yon turnip lands seeming as littered with gold.
　'Tis the charlock in blossom, a troublesome weed,
　Yet a beautiful sight in the distance indeed.
They are nought for a nosegay yet still in fine weather
　You see what a show they make growing together.
　Aye, yonder are steeples that catch on the eye
　Like giants of stone stretching up to the sky,
And windmills are sweeping their sails up and down
And cottages peeping all sunny and brown—
　See the cows grazing yonder and less quiet sheep,
　Some at feed and some chewing their cuds till they sleep.
Thus the prospect in varied profusions abound
And spreadeth a beautiful picture around,
　Though there shines no old ruins for artists to prize
　Nor mountains to thrust up their heads to the skies,
Yet as like DeWint's pictures as nature can be,
For nature owns no sweeter painter than he.

Nay, don't be alarmed and start up from the hay,
That's nought but a little mouse running away,
And now she finds out we're not foes to destroy,
Do but hear in the grass how she chitters for joy.
  No doubt in the beans nigh at hand may sojourn
  Her children awaiting their mother's return.
See out there where the willow bends over the brook
At our feet like an old shepherd over his crook.
  'Neath its boughs gnats and midges are still at their play
  Like ballrooms of fairies all dancing away.
Aye, there in rich dress goes the grand dragonfly
Like another proud thing buzzing scornfully by.
  He scarce turns his head on their dancing and glee
  And they're as full careless of notice as he.
O don't you, my Anna, be cruel and vain.
The smallest of things are not strangers to pain.
  That long-legged shepherd you've caught, let him go!
  For he knows naught at all what you threaten, no, no!
Though you'll tell him you'll kill both his son and his daughter
If he will not afford you a small drop of water,
  Your threats and your language he can't understand,
  Though he sheds tears for freedom while shut in your hand.
And here's little Freddy crying "click clocking clay."
Poh! Ladybirds know not the time of the day,
  Of "one o'clock, two o'clock," no such a thing—
  So give it its freedom and let it take wing.
Well, now if you're rested, we'll wander again,
Here the path strides the brook over closes of grain.
  So who's first to venture? Come, never see fear,

Though the plank bends beneath, no danger is near.
Well, if you are fearful, we'll turn back and go
Where stepping-stones ford o'er a shallow below.
  Danger's seldom, my children, so near as we think
  And often seems far when we stand on the brink,
As the runlet in shallows bawls loud and in deeps
Deceitfully slips into silence and sleeps.
  Do but try how delicious these bean-blossoms smell.
No flower in the garden delights me so well,
Perfuming the nest of the partridge that lies
Basking safe in the shadows their forest supplies.
  And the hare — here's a beaten path tracks her retreat —
  Feels timidly safe in her corn-covered seat.
On this mown baulk, no doubt she oft ventures to play
When a grasshopper's rustle might fright her away.
  How sweet and how happy such places appear!
  Well indeed may you wish that our cottage were here
With the wild bees for neighbors the whole summer long
And the lark ever near us a-piping his song
  And the beans in full blossom close up to our door
  And cows in the distance at feed on the moor
And grasshoppers singing where'er we might roam
And partridges calling at night by our home,
  Where we might sit at eve in our parlor and see
  The rabbit bob out from that old hollow tree,
And hear from yon thicket so gloomy and deep
The sweet little nightingale sing us to sleep,
  Which he heard t'other night — don't you recollect now.
  When I clomb the wood stile to get each one a bough,
How one sung "jug jug" and you all sung amain
"Jug jug" and laughed loud as it answered again?
  Aye, aye, I knew well such a beautiful song
  Would not be so quickly forgot. Come along,
For the day gets so hot you may well wish again
To meet with the coolness we left in the lane.
  Do but look at our shadows: what strangers we've got!

Those giants that came with us first from our cot
Stalking on stride for stride in a pomp-stirring mood,
Nigh as tall as the oaks that lay peeled by the wood,
  Whose long legs might cross a brook ever so wide
  And leap o'er a hedge, nay a house, at a stride,
They've left us and shrunk from our sight by degrees
To children and dwarfs scarce as high as our knees,
  Then as we go on shrink so close to our feet,
  As if they were glad to get out of the heat.
Come, here is the footpath that leads to the town.
Don't stop — 'tis so hot, loves — we cannot sit down.
  O I see what delights ye — aye, climb on the stile
  And look round about as ye wish for a while.
Those things that go sweeing away to the wind,
Though the willows scarce move that are growing behind,
  Are the sails of the mill, and indeed, as you say,
  They follow each other like things in their play,
Now dropping, then rising their wearisome round
And seem where you stand to spring out of the ground.
  Yon shepherd boy doubtless thinks so, as he lies
  Lolling o'er the gate gazing in happy surprise.
See, now they move slower. The wind's nearly still,
And there comes the miller — look — out of his mill
  To peep at the weather with meal powdered o'er,
  More white than the dog-rose in bloom by the door.
See, there goes the mower a-sweeping away,
And yon folks in the nook — see — are stacking of hay,
  Some loading, some forking. The grounds are alive
  With their labor, as busy as bees in a hive.
There's no one seems idle but this little boy
Who runs after butterflies bawling for joy,
  And now he has run like a fox in the wheat.
  (If the farmer came by he would surely get beat.)
The partridge whirs up frit away from her nest
And the hare with the morning dew wet on her breast
  Jumps away from his hustle and bustle and noise

Which he makes in the midst of his raptures and joys,
Now singing and tearing up weeds of all sorts,
Showy corn poppies shining like foxhunters' coats
  And bluecaps and cockleflowers, no matter what,
  To make a gay garland to stick in his hat.
And now he stands out. What a gesture he wears,
As proud of his colors as soldiers of theirs,
  And why may he not be as vain as the rest?
  Of proud folk the proudest have baubles at best.
Yes, summer indeed brings the pleasure to all.
That colt feels its freedom now loosed from its stall,
  And even the wearisome wayfaring ass
  Can find on the common his bunches of grass
While round the warped camp 'neath yon bushes and trees
The gypsies lie basking themselves at their ease
  And the gypsy boys shaking their rags at the sun
  Are head over ears in their frolic and fun,
Chasing barefoot along with their dogs by their side
Barking loud as the rabbits bob by them to hide.
  See there sit the swath summer lovers at play
  'Neath the shade of those wide-spreading maples all day,
Those brown tawny lasses with lips like a cherry
And hair full as dark as the autumn blackberry.
  The mole hillocks make them soft cushions for love
  And the hedges in arbors hang blooming above.
As blessed as the rich who on sofas repose,
They toy 'neath the shades of wild woodbine and rose.
  Now look at the sky—it grows muddy with showers
  And black snails are creeping about in the flowers.
The daisy too. Look, 'tis a good weather-glass.
It seems even now half-asleep in the grass
  And other flowers too, like the sun on the wane,
  Are shutting their eyes and seem dreaming again,
While the shepherd boy yonder is startled from sleep,
Peeping up at the sky as he bawls to his sheep.
  No doubt he is seeking his hut by the hedge

All wattled with willows and covered with sedge
To lie on his bed of cut brakes and be dry
While the threatened approach of the storm lessens by.
   Now I see you are glad to get sight of the town.
   See, there's the old spire and below it — look down —
Our cottage is peeping, aye, now you see't plain
As if it was happy to find us again,
   And happy am I we're so nigh to the door,
   So run in and take to your play as before,
Or rest in your chairs from the toils of the day
By the oak bough that looms in the chimney so gay.
   See there — waning sunbeams, they twitter and fall
   Through the diamond-paned window to dance on the wall.
The pictures seem smiling its glitter to court
And up jumps the kitten to join in the sport.
   Aye, well may you say you are glad we've got home,
   For sweeter it seemeth the farther we roam.
So now we'll sit down and enjoy at our ease
The rest leisure gives us and do as we please.
   Take your toys or read lessons and chatter between
   Of the walk we have had and the things we have seen,
And while you are pleasing or resting yourselves,
I'll reach down a poet I love from the shelves,
   My Thomson and Cowper like flowers in their prime
   That sat not in closets to study and rhyme
But roamed out of doors for their verses that yield
A freshness like that which we left in the field,
   That sings both at once to the ear and the eye
   And breathes of the air and the grass and the sky
A music so sweet while we're hid from the rain
That we even seem taking our rambles again.

SUMMER EVENING

The frog, half-fearful, jumps across the path,
And little mouse that leaves its hole at eve
Nimbles with timid dread beneath the swath.
My rustling steps awhile their joys deceive
Till past, and then the cricket sings more strong
And grasshoppers in merry moods still wear
The short night weary with their fretting song.
Up from behind the molehill jumps the hare,
Cheat of its chosen bed, and from the bank
The yellowhammer flutters in short fears
From off its nest, hid in the grasses rank,
And drops again when no more noise it hears.
Thus nature's human link and endless thrall:
Proud man still seems the enemy of all.

A Walk

The thorn tree juſt began to bud
  And greening ſtained the sheltering hedge
And many a violet 'side the wood
  Peeped blue between the withered sedge.
The sun gleamed warm the bank beside,
  'Twas pleasant wandering out awhile
'Neath neſtling bush to lonely hide
  Or bend in musing o'er a ſtile.

I wandered down the narrow lane
  Whose battered paths were hardly dry
And to the wild heath went again
  Upon its wilderness to lie,
There mixed with joy that never tires,
  Far from the busy hum of men,
Among its molehills, furze and briars,
  Then further ſtrolled and dropped again.

GLOSSARY

The publisher of the very firſt edition of Clare's poems, *Poems De-scriptive of Rural Life and Scenery*, in 1820, included a glossary of his dialect words. We've done the same and included some botanical and ornithological terms. Sources: Clare, Poems, 1820; Clare, The Village Minſtrel, 1822; James Barclay, A Complete and Universal English Dictionary, 1795; Oxford English Dictionary; Joesph Wright, The English Dialect Dictionary, 1903; Clare, Major Works, ed. Eric Robinson and David Powell, Oxford; Clare, "I Am": The Selected Poetry, ed. Jonathan Bate, Farrar, Straus & Giroux.

ash-dotterel   A "dotterel" is, according to OED, "a doddered tree," and for "doddered," a dialect word applied to oaks and other hardwoods signifying a tree in its dotage
balks   narrow ſtrips of grass dividing two fields
bashed   bashful
baulk   a narrow ſtrip of grass dividing two ploughed fields
blea   cold, chilly wind (Barclay). Oxford: "bleak, wild, exposed"
brake   fern, bracken
briony or *bryony*   cucumber family; the only English species, *bryonia dioica*, has a white five-petaled flower and grows in hedgerows
carlock or *charlock*   *sinapsis arvensis*, field muſtard
cat-gallows   a children's jumping game, of two ſticks ſtuck vertically in the ground with a third laid across the top, shaped like a gallows
cesspools   pools of rainwater from a peat dig (Bate)
chaffinch   *fringilla coelebs*, a very common bird of field and farmyard
click clocking clay   A "clock o' clay" is a ladybird. The expression seems to refer to a children's game to do with the insect
closen   small fields
closes   small fields or enclosures
corn   grain
corn-fields   fields of grain

cot   cottage

Cowper   William Cowper (1731-1800), English poet, author of *The Task*

craking   "continual fretting and complaining, persistent chatter" (Wright)

crimping   adj. "crimped or curled in minute creases" (OED)

dewberry   *rubus ceasisus*, same family as the blackberry; dark, sweet fruit and broad leaves

DeWint   Peter DeWint (1784-1849), English landscape painter

dottrel   "old stumping tree in hedge-rows that are headed every ten or twelve years for firewood," Clare's note. OED: decayed, old

drabbled   "wet with dirty water" (OED)

firetail   *ruticilla phoenicurus* According to W.H. Hudson's *British Birds*, "a common name for the redstart."

flag-leaf   the last leaf to open on a wheat plant as it ripens

frit   frightened

furze   *ulex europaeus*, gorse, "a spiny evergreen shrub with yellow flower growing abundantly in waste lands" and a very old word in English

gadding   given to roving or gadding about

Goody   traditional name for a farm wife

hedge-sparrow   *prunella modularis*, also called dunnock

knapping   biting with the teeth, nibbling

ladybird   U.S., ladybug

leveret   "a young hare, strictly one in its first year" (OED)

linnet   *carduelis cannabina*, house finch

long-legged shepherd   crane-fly, *tipula paludosa*; U.S., daddy long-legs

old man's beard   *clematis vitalba*, a native British wildflower, it produces greenish-white, very fragrant flowers in summer and attractive, feathery seed heads in fall

osiers   twigs from a willow

Parnassus Hill   Mount Parnassus in Greece. In mythology, the home of the muses

pink   dialect name for the chaffinch, whose song is *pink pink pink* (OED)

pip or *peep*   single blossom of a flower growing in a cluster

pismires   ants

pooties   snails or snail shells "girdled snail shell, *helix nemoralis*"

posey or *posy*   "a short motto, originally a line or verse of poetry and usually in patterned language, inscribed on a knife within a ring, as a heraldic motto." Also: "an emblem, or emblematic device." Also "a bouquet of flowers (*rustic*)" and "a collection or bouquet of 'flowers' of poetry or rhetoric." (OED)

prankt   "dressed in a gay, bright, or showy manner" (OED)

prog   poke

puddock   *milvus milvus*, kite

pudge   puddle

ramp "*of plants*   to climb, chiefly *dial,*; of non-climbing plants, to grow rankly and luxuriantly, now *dial*." (OED)

rill   a brook, rivulet

shapen   v. "*rare*, to shape, impart a shape to." (OED)

shoy   shy

sooth   as an adj. "*poet*., soothing, soft, smooth" (OED cites Keats)

sprents   sprinkles

stile   "an arrangement of steps, rungs, or the like, contrived to allow passage over or through a fence to one person at a time, while forming a barrier to the passage of sheep or cattle" (OED)

stinking finweed   *onanis repens*, the other common name is "rest harrow"

sturt or *sturtle*   startle, move suddenly

swail   shade

swath or *swarth*   grassland, turf

swee   a dialect form of "sway"

swopping   pouncing (Clare's citation. OED gives both "swooping" and "sweeping")

taste   the usage meaning, "a style or manner exhibiting aesthetic discernment" (OED), came into use in the middle of the 18th century

ted   "to spread out, scatter, or strew abroadf (new-mown grass) for drying." (OED)

Thomson   James Thomson (1700-1784), Scottish poet, author of *The Seasons*

trotty wagtail   *motacilla alba*, the pied wagtail, a sprightly black and white bird

warped   built up by deposits of soil from a current of water *whimpling*   rippling, meandering

white-throat   *Sylvia communis*, a small gray-brown warbler with a
pinkish breast and a white throat, a garden bird

yellowhammer   *emberiza citronella*, a sparrow-like field bird with a
yellow head

TITLE INDEX

ACKNOWLEDGMENTS

A book certainly becomes a collaboration once in the publishers hands, and one always hopes and prays for a good editor and designer to work alongside. I always feel a little lost and less confident without the two. A deep bow of gratitude, I thank Jack Shoemaker for his immediate enthusiasm for this project and his direction in helping to shape this book. I thank David Bullen who framed the poems and artwork on these pages with such impeccable design. It was a treat to work again with the two of them.

I thank Bob Hass for the herculean task of editing the punctuation in Clare's poems, and for his superb introduction. I felt the book become all the more real in his hands. The numerous emails we exchanged while tracking down definitions for the glossary was especially fun.

I thank Simon Kovesi of Oxford Brookes University, and editor of the *John Clare Society Journal,* for publishing several of my sketches, and for his kind words of encouragement when this book was first brewing in my head.

A special thanks too goes to David Aldera at New York Central Art Supply, for turning up such beautiful, vintage handmade watercolor papers over the years. A friend and mentor.

Printed in the United States
by Baker & Taylor Publisher Services